American
CULTURE & CONFLICT

Living Through THE CIVIL RIGHTS MOVEMENT

Linden McNeilly

Rourke
Educational Media
rourkeeducationalmedia.com

Before & After Reading Activities

Before Reading:

Building Academic Vocabulary and Background Knowledge

Before reading a book, it is important to tap into what your child or students already know about the topic. This will help them develop their vocabulary, increase their reading comprehension, and make connections across the curriculum.

1. *Look at the cover of the book. What will this book be about?*
2. *What do you already know about the topic?*
3. *Let's study the Table of Contents. What will you learn about in the book's chapters?*
4. *What would you like to learn about this topic? Do you think you might learn about it from this book? Why or why not?*
5. *Use a reading journal to write about your knowledge of this topic. Record what you already know about the topic and what you hope to learn about the topic.*
6. *Read the book.*
7. *In your reading journal, record what you learned about the topic and your response to the book.*
8. *After reading the book complete the activities below.*

Content Area Vocabulary

Read the list. What do these words mean?

designated
eligible
forbade
integrate
mutilated
propel
retaliation
rift
segregated
unanimous

After Reading:

Comprehension and Extension Activity

After reading the book, work on the following questions with your child or students in order to check their level of reading comprehension and content mastery.

1. *Describe at least two events that were considered key to starting or energizing the Civil Rights era. (Summarize)*
2. *When school districts closed down to avoid integration, what can you infer the school leaders cared about most? (Infer)*
3. *Think of two questions you'd ask Rosa Parks about her decision to stay seated on the bus. (Asking Questions)*
4. *Have you ever assumed someone is better than you before you know him or her? Describe the situation. (Text to Self Connection)*
5. *Think of two questions you could ask a state trooper who was ordered to prevent black teens from attending an all-white school. (Asking Questions)*

Extension Activity

Imagine you are a young person during the Civil Rights movement. Write a personal narrative about your experiences, including at least two real events (even if they are in different time periods). Tell your story to the class or a small group, and be ready to answer questions from your classmates as though you are that person.

TABLE OF CONTENTS

KEY EVENTS

May 17, 1954:	The U.S. Supreme Court outlaws segregation in public schools with Brown v. Board of Education decision
1955 to 1957:	Bus boycott in Montgomery, Alabama, organized by Dr. Martin Luther King, Jr. and set off by Rosa Parks
1963:	Reports and images of Birmingham, Alabama, police using dogs and fire hoses on black demonstrators increase public support for civil rights movement
August 28, 1963:	Martin Luther King, Jr. gives his "I Have a Dream" speech during the March on Washington
July 2, 1964:	President Lyndon B. Johnson signs the Civil Rights Act
1965:	Martin Luther King, Jr. leads march from Selma to Montgomery, Alabama, calling for black voter registration
August 6, 1965:	President Lyndon B. Johnson signs the Voting Rights Act
April 4, 1968:	Martin Luther King, Jr. is assassinated, setting off riots in more than 100 cities across the U.S.

CHAPTER ONE

LIVING THROUGH THE CIVIL RIGHTS ERA

The Civil Rights Era was a time of turmoil. Efforts to change society were met by great resistance. Those who lived through it saw many things: peaceful protest and violent actions, solemn marches and fiery speeches, law enforcement both protecting citizens and attacking them. There was murder, terrorism, inspiration, and dedication.

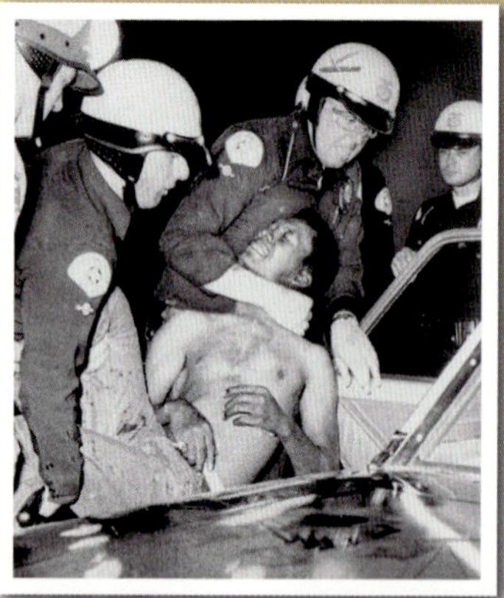

Police arrest a man during the 1965 Watts Riots in Los Angeles.

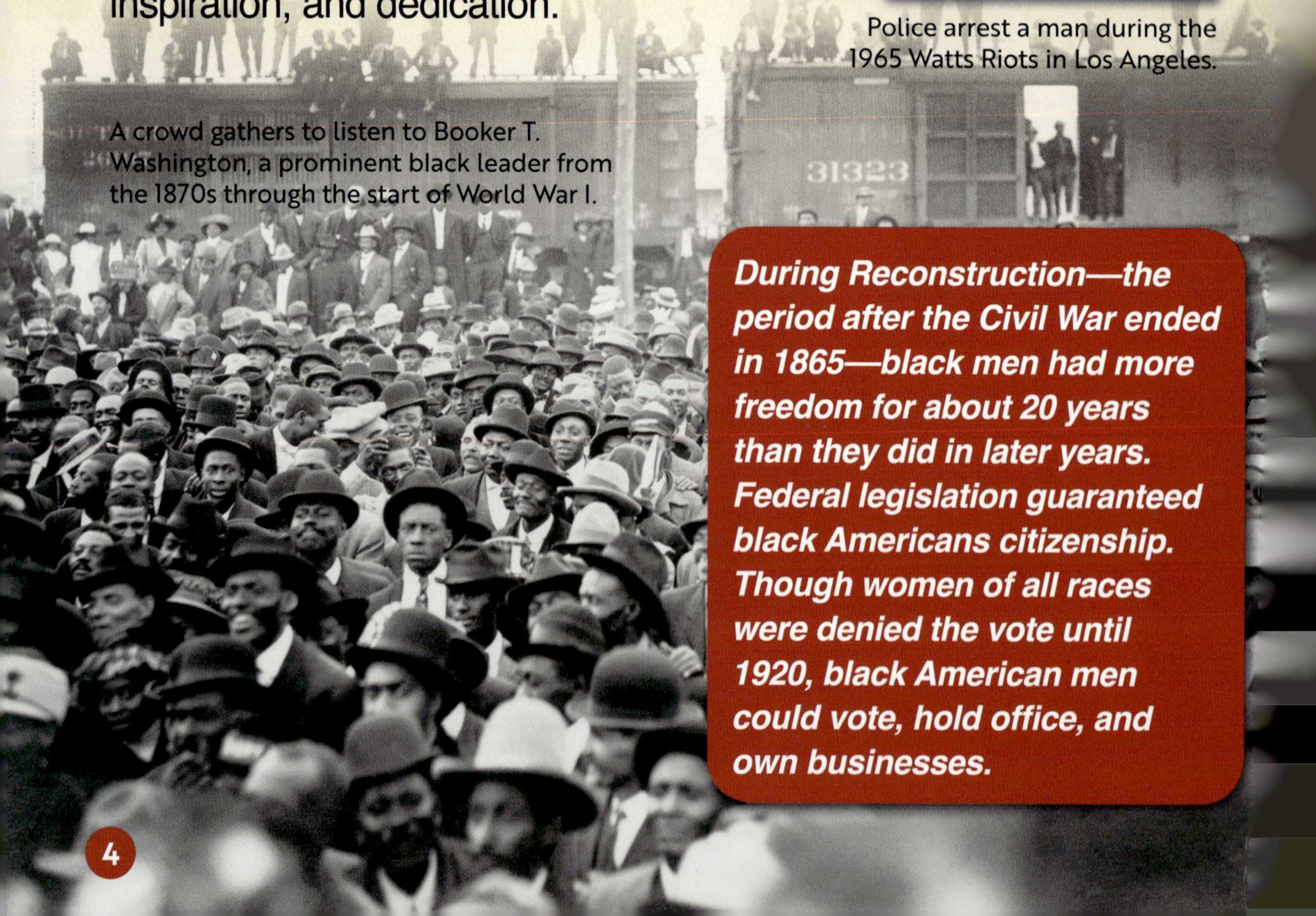

A crowd gathers to listen to Booker T. Washington, a prominent black leader from the 1870s through the start of World War I.

During Reconstruction—the period after the Civil War ended in 1865—black men had more freedom for about 20 years than they did in later years. Federal legislation guaranteed black Americans citizenship. Though women of all races were denied the vote until 1920, black American men could vote, hold office, and own businesses.

The Civil Rights Movement took place mostly between 1951 and 1970. Its root was the large **rift** between the rights stated in the Constitution and the rights minority Americans, particularly black Americans, actually had.

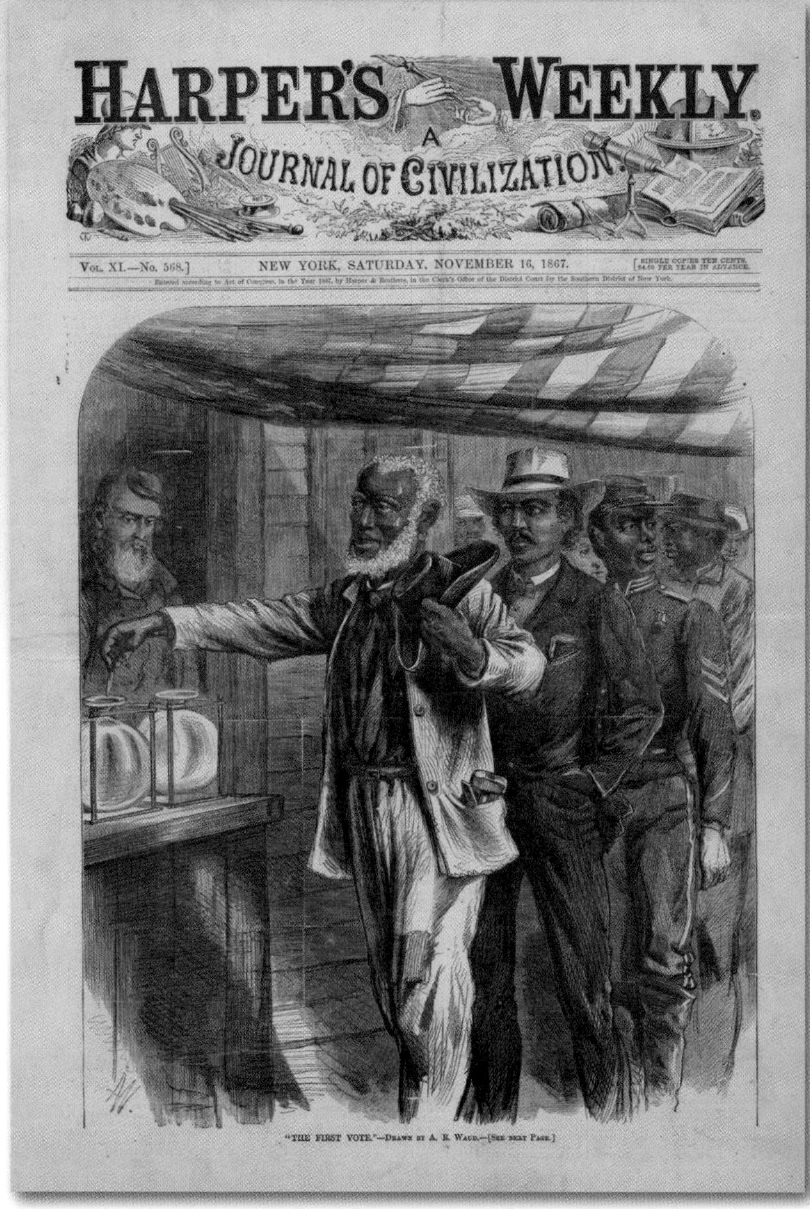

A magazine illustration shows men lined up to vote.

An officer sits outside a separate entrance for black military police.

By the end of the 1800s, white legislators in the southern states had reduced the freedoms given to black people. They passed laws limiting where black people could go, what jobs they could do, and changed rules about voting. They charged voters a tax, which many low-income black citizens couldn't afford.

Even waiting rooms in public areas were divided into "White" and "Colored."

Some state governments followed the 1896 Supreme Court ruling referred to as "separate but equal." This ruling in the Plessy v. Ferguson case said that racially separate facilities, if equal, did not violate the Constitution. But the judges that made that decision were white men who never felt its negative effects. It took many decades, but eventually it was proved that separate could never be equal.

Restrooms and water fountains were marked "white" and "colored" as a result of Jim Crow laws.

Education, housing, transportation, and even access to buildings and drinking fountains were **segregated** by race. Black people had to use back entrances to many public buildings, and sit in separate waiting areas. These laws were called Jim Crow.

CHAPTER TWO

SEPARATE IS NOT EQUAL

Under Jim Crow, black and white people had different educations. In 1951, Barbara Johns, a 16-year-old at all-black Moton High School in Prince Edward County, Virginia, disliked the poor quality of the education she and other black students were receiving.

R. R. Moton High School is considered "the student birthplace of America's Civil Rights Movement."

The Virginia Civil Rights Memorial in Richmond, Virginia, is a monument to the protests that led to the end of school segregation in the state.

Some classes were held in a bus or in tar paper shacks, and they lacked the equipment and funds the white high school had. Johns decided to lead her 450 classmates in a two-week walkout.

Students at Moton High called the tar paper shacks "chicken coops" because they were rough, temporary buildings. Students held umbrellas to keep rainwater from ruining their papers. Smoke filled the room from the pot-bellied stoves used for heat. But the white high school was made of brick, with modern heating.

Students work in a classroom at R.R. Moton High School in 1951.

Johns asked the National Association for the Advancement of Colored People for legal aid for Moton High School. Eventually, the NAACP brought five cases together to form the lawsuit called Brown v. Board of Education. It was one of the most important Supreme Court decisions ever considered.

Vivian Malone Jones became one of the first black students to enroll at the University of Alabama in 1963.

After a year and a half of hearings and deliberations, in May of 1954, the Supreme Court issued the **unanimous** decision that in education, separate is never equal. Across the nation, the media spread the news.

By 1957, many classes were integrated, like this one at Anacostia High School in Washington, D. C.

Many were happy that the court had stood up for equality. But the ruling was only the beginning. There were still many years and efforts—marches, sit-ins, speeches, and more lawsuits—required to actually turn the decision into law.

Alabama Governor George Wallace is confronted by Deputy U.S. Attorney General Nicholas Katzenbach as he tries to block integration at the University of Alabama.

When black students tried to attend white-only schools, they were met with violence, hatred, and local resistance. Some locals and southern leaders insisted it was too soon or too hard to **integrate** schools.

The National Guard sent armed escort to make sure the nine African-American high school students could safely enroll in Central High School.

In September 1957, nine black students tried to attend all-white Central High School in Little Rock, Arkansas. But the governor sent law enforcement to prevent them from entering. The students were met with cruelty and violence for days. Finally, President Dwight Eisenhower sent federal troops to protect the teens.

For young people in the South, school was often disrupted. Some school boards simply closed schools rather than allow black students to attend. White students could often attend private schools, but black students had to find other ways to get education. These included moving to relatives' homes, entering the foster care system, or being taught at home.

CHAPTER THREE

JUSTICE: NOT FOR EVERYONE

Lynching is a kind of terrorism, often done by mobs. If a mob decided someone (often a black person) had done something wrong, they took the law into their hands and killed—or "lynched"—them. The most common way to kill was by hanging.

Mary Burnett Talbert worked tirelessly to fight lynching. She was the national director of the NAACP Anti-Lynching Campaign in 1921.

A mob of white men gather around the victims of a lynching in Minnesota in 1920. It was common for photos of lynchings to circulate, or even be sent as postcards.

Between 1882 and 1968, more than 4,700 known lynching murders occurred in the United States. About 75 percent of the victims were black. This number represents only documented lynchings. Some historians think the true total is much higher.

Laura and L. D. Nelson, an African-American mother and her teenage son, were lynched from this bridge in May 1911. They had been jailed for allegedly attacking the local sheriff. A mob seized and hung them from a railroad bridge over the North Canadian River.

White people often went free after lynching black people, who could be murdered for very small actions. Many southern black parents told their children to always follow rules so as not to draw the anger and potential deadly force of the white people in power.

A gruesome lynching energized the Civil Rights Movement. In 1955, 14-year-old Emmett Till was visiting relatives in Money, Mississippi. He bragged about having a white girlfriend back in Chicago. Other teens dared him to ask a white storeowner, Carolyn Bryant, for a date.

Bryant's Grocery and Meat Market, which offered service to local African Americans, went broke in a little more than a year after Roy Bryant's murder trial. Many local African Americans boycotted both the stores of the two men who were tried for murdering Emmett Till.

Emmett couldn't back down, so he bought some gum, said, "Goodbye," and allegedly whistled at Carolyn as he left the store. Carolyn's husband and brother-in-law, Roy Bryant and J. W. Milam, kidnapped Emmett at gunpoint. They beat him and murdered him, and threw his body in a river.

Emmett Till's body was found in the Tallahatchie River.

Carolyn Bryant testified in court that Emmett had put his hands on her hips and said crude things to her. This made the jury angry when they heard it. But in 2017, it was revealed that she had invented that testimony.

Emmett's great uncle, Moses Wright, holds Emmett's clothing. He testified at the murder trial even though it put his own life in danger.

It was considered daring when Mose Wright, Emmett's great uncle, and two other black relatives took the stand to testify against Roy Bryant and J. W. Milam. Blacks could be killed for testifying against whites.

Emmett Till, nicknamed "Bobo," poses with his mother, Mamie, before traveling to Mississippi in 1955.

The all-white jury returned a "not guilty" verdict. Nationally, papers were filled with the news, blasting the verdict as unfair and un-American. The two murderers, who later confessed to a journalist, went free.

*When Emmett's **mutilated** body was sent home to his mother, she had an open casket funeral to show the world what had happened. News photos of the gruesome sight helped **propel** the Civil Rights Movement forward. Black Americans were urged to vote, get new local law enforcement, and work for justice for all.*

CHAPTER FOUR

HALT THE BUSES!

In Montgomery, Alabama, everyday life was controlled by segregation. Schools, restaurants, movie theaters, public water fountains, and seating on public buses were divided into black and white areas. Black passengers paid bus drivers at the front, and then entered at the rear.

Lawmakers made the rules of segregation and police enforced it.

Waiting rooms in bus and train stations were labeled by skin color.

Customers had to select the entrance based on skin color, even though it led to the same place.

In December of 1955, ten weeks after Emmett Till's murder, Rosa Parks was seated in the back part of a public bus. When the bus filled, she didn't give her seat to a white passenger, as the law required.

Rosa Parks
(1913 - 2005)

The bus driver had her arrested. Rosa wasn't surprised. She'd been arrested for breaking another bus law years earlier. Rosa had training in antidiscrimination work. She and other civil rights leaders knew her arrest could serve as a test case to break segregation in Montgomery.

The arrest began the 381-day Montgomery bus boycott. Forty thousand black citizens refused to ride the buses. All of them found other ways to get around for a year. Eventually, businesses had lost millions in sales, and the bus company had to raise fares and limit routes.

The bus Rosa Parks rode in when she was arrested now sits in a museum.

Police officer Lt. D. H. Lackey fingerprints Rosa Parks on February 22, 1956. She was arrested along with about a hundred other people for violating segregation laws during the bus boycott.

Reverend Martin Luther King, Jr. was 26 when he organized the bus boycott. He promoted the concept of peaceful resistance, saying, "If you protest courageously, and yet with dignity and Christian love...the historians will have to say, 'There lived a great people—a black people—who injected new meaning and dignity into the veins of civilization.'"

An African-American woman is arrested in Montgomery, Alabama.

Montgomery Mayor W. A. Gayle publically blamed black people, who were fired from jobs and treated with violence. Even when the Supreme Court ruled that segregation was unconstitutional, bombings and threats continued.

CHAPTER FIVE

A SEAT AT THE TABLE

In February of 1960, four black freshmen from North Carolina Agricultural and Technical College went into a Woolworth's store in Greensboro, purchased a few items, then sat down at the lunch counter **designated** for white people.

The building that once housed the old Woolworth lunch counter is now the International Civil Rights Museum & Center in Greensboro, North Carolina. The lunch counter is on display there.

The four asked for service, but were denied. They returned the next day, and the day after that. The "Greensboro Four," joined by friends and supporters, returned to the Woolworth's lunch counter daily for six months. Service continued to be refused.

James Lawson, a student at Vanderbilt University conducting nonviolent workshops said, "Do show yourself friendly on the counter at all times. Do sit straight and always face the counter. Don't strike back, or curse back if attacked. Don't laugh out. Don't hold conversations. Don't block entrances … Remember the teachings of Jesus, Gandhi, Martin Luther King."

James Lawson (shown here in 2005) has spent much of his life leading people to non-violent protest. While enrolled in Vanderbilt University in 1959-1960 he helped lead the lunch room sit-ins in Nashville, Tennessee. He was expelled from the university for this, but went on supporting and training people in non-violent protest for many years.

This nonviolent protest of segregation got a lot of attention. The movement soon spread to 54 cities in nine states. Young black people were entering lunch counters and demanding equal treatment. Tensions in local communities raised.

For black Americans living during the Civil Rights Movement, it took courage to do what many think nothing of today: sit at a lunch counter as an equal with a white person.

Simply sitting was an act of courage and strength in the face of bullies like these boys in Virginia.

Money in his hand, college student Benjamin Cowins tries to get service at a McCrory's lunch counter in Tallahassee, Florida on February 21, 1961. He looks toward the waitress, who is ignoring him. Two weeks later he was arrested at a Neisners lunch counter, which led to his spending 30 days in jail.

White hecklers poured hot coffee, sugar, and ketchup on the sitters. Police beat them with billy clubs and set police dogs on them even when the protestors did nothing. But the news media published images of violence, and people across the country took notice.

The sit-in movement grew to include some 70,000 people across the country. In July 1960, the Woolworth's counter was open to all races. Other stores and restaurants soon opened their businesses to all races, as well. The Greensboro Woolworth's building became the site of the International Civil Rights Center & Museum in 2010. The lunch counter remains as a tribute to the bravery and determination of the peaceful protesters.

CHAPTER SIX

LONG TRIP TO FREEDOM

One method of making a difference was to participate in peaceful protests. These happened mostly in the South. But northern cities such as New York, Chicago, and Boston also had protests, along with many college campuses.

Statues of notable protestors inside the National Civil Rights Museum in Memphis, Tennessee.

Protestors practiced nonviolence. They did not resist arrest or fight back when police or citizens attacked them. They were determined to remain calm, which took great will power and inner strength. Many historians believe that the nonviolence of the movement helped the protestors gain support from the general population.

Protestors chose public places to speak and stand together. They wanted others to hear what they had to say and understand why laws should be changed. Some passersby insulted or attacked them, but others joined in and supported them.

If put in jail, protestors adopted the policy of "jail not bail." Rather than pay the bail to be released, they stayed in jail. This created more work for law enforcement and got more attention.

Replica of jail cell where Dr. Martin Luther King, Jr. was held. Located at the National Civil Rights Museum in Memphis, Tennessee.

People march from New York City to Washington, D.C., to participate in the March on Washington in 1963.

Civil rights leaders chose a nationwide march to bring attention to the need for a Civil Rights Act, integration of all schools, and better employment policies for minorities. Civil rights groups and church groups throughout the country publicized the march.

The March on Washington was one of the largest political rallies for human rights in American history at the time.

King delivers his famous speech.

More than 250,000 Americans, mostly black but many white, went to Washington, D. C. on August 28, 1963, to demand change. Many speakers and singers offered hope and strength, but the most famous speech was Rev. Martin Luther King, Jr.'s "I Have a Dream," which added emotional urgency to passing Civil Rights legislation.

President Kennedy meets with his staff to discuss actions to take on civil rights.

President John F. Kennedy had proposed a Civil Rights bill, but was assassinated before it passed. President Lyndon B. Johnson took it up and made changes, using JFK's legacy as a selling point.

President Lyndon B. Johnson meets with Martin Luther King Jr., Whitney Young, and James Farmer at the White House in 1964.

The bill survived 60 days of filibuster, an effort to keep the bill from passing used by the senators who disagreed with it. The new law outlawed segregation in schools, jobs, and housing and established equal employment opportunity.

President John F. Kennedy stands with Senator Clair Engle.

To vote "yes" on legislation, senators say "yay" as their names are called. But when California Senator Clair Engle's name was called, he couldn't respond due to a brain tumor that robbed him of speech. Instead, he slowly raised his hand to point to his eye, meaning "aye," another form of "yes." Senator Engle died not long after.

In the early 1960s, children show enthusiasm for voting as they stand by a voter registration table and sign reminding citizens to register.

Next, civil rights leaders decided to focus on voter rights. Only two million of the South's five million **eligible** black voters were registered. Workers focused on Selma, Alabama, because of the extremely low percentage of black voters there.

African Americans and whites voting together.

Many black citizens were afraid to register to vote. Local papers often published names of those who "dared" to register, making them targets for* retaliation *by their bosses or landlords. When some lined up to register to vote, the local sheriff took photos of them to frighten and harass them.

Voting officials, primarily in southern states, had been known to make it very hard for black citizens to register to vote. Some had to recite the entire Constitution or explain complicated parts of state laws. Even black people with college degrees were turned away.

Locals view the bomb-damaged home of Arthur Shores, NAACP attorney, in Birmingham, Alabama. Shores's wife was injured in the bombing.

Though federal law said all races could use buses, trains, and terminals together, the states had rules of their own, forcing the races to stay separate in terminal restrooms, restaurants, and waiting rooms as well as on the buses.

In 1961, the Freedom Riders stopped at this former Greyhound bus station in Montgomery, Alabama and were attacked by protesters.

In 1961, seven black people and six white people left Washington, D.C. to travel together on Greyhound and Trailways buses into the South. They wanted to challenge states with laws that controlled bus and station segregation.

In 1961, civil rights leaders devised a plan to have a group of black and white people travel together by bus from Washington, D.C., into the South, using the terminals and facilities as equals.

Freedom Riders headed to Tallahassee, Florida were arrested.

Their trip was mostly untroubled until they reached Alabama. An angry mob of 200 surrounded one bus, smashing windows and burning the bus to the ground. The riders escaped with their lives, and the photo of the burning bus was on the front page of most newspapers across the country the next day.

The burning bus from the Mother's Day attack in Birmingham, Alabama.

On Mother's Day, May 14, an angry mob surrounded a second busload of Freedom Riders arriving in Birmingham, Alabama. They pulled riders off the bus, beating them until they were bloody or unconscious. No police came to protect the riders.

Historic plaque dedicated to the Freedom Riders located in downtown Birmingham.

When questioned why no police came to restore order, Birmingham's Public Safety Commissioner Bull Connor said most were visiting their mothers. Later it was discovered that the police promised to stay away so that hate groups could beat the Freedom Riders.

Though the Freedom Riders were peaceful, they were seized by mobs and beaten.

Civil rights leaders meet with President John F. Kennedy in the Oval Office of the White House after the March on Washington, D.C.

By the third attack on the bus riders, President Kennedy took action. Alabama's governor would not protect the riders. Kennedy sent hundreds of troops to protect the bus riders. Throughout the summer, Freedom Riders rode on, and got arrested. The federal government finally enforced regulations that prohibited racist policies in interstate travel.

Dr. Martin Luther King, Jr. and the Abernathy family join others to lead the march from Selma, Alabama to Montgomery in March of 1965.

On February 18, 1965, Jimmie Lee Jackson, a 26-year-old civil rights marcher, was shot by an Alabama State Trooper. When he died, angry organizers planned a 50-mile (80.5 kilometer) march from Selma to Montgomery to protest to Governor George Wallace, who immediately **forbade** the march.

Leaders always urged calm and control during marches.

State troopers fired tear gas and set attack dogs on the marchers, who had to turn back. National news media showed Americans the brutality. By March 21, the march started again. It grew to some 25,000 people by the time they reached the capital city.

After the march, President Johnson moved forward with the Voting Rights Act, which lifted the states' restrictions on black people, making it easier to register and vote. It vastly improved voter turnout. In Mississippi alone, voter turnout among black citizens increased from six percent in 1964 to 59 percent in 1969.

CHAPTER SIX

A BETTER WORLD

The Civil Rights Movement accomplished important things. It confronted the unfair rules that separated black and white Americans, showed the American public the truth about how black Americans were treated, and pushed the federal government to make real change in laws.

The Foot Soldier Statue by Ronald S. McDowell shows a youth being attacked by a police dog. It symbolizes the many Americans who suffered attacks by dogs, spray of fire hoses, police beatings and other assaults as they exercised the right to pursue justice. It stands in Kelly Ingram Park in Birmingham, Alabama.

March on Washington, 1963.

Marchers protest the bombing of 16th Street Baptist Church, an African American church, which killed four girls and injured 22 others. Four members of the Ku Klux Klan planted dynamite set on a timer on the church steps. It took many years for the murderers to be brought to justice.

It took courage, effort, patience, and sometimes loss of lives, including that of Dr. Martin Luther King, Jr. in 1968, to bring about social change. Though many of the events were public and dramatic, others were slow and quiet, one lawsuit or formal complaint at a time.

U.S. Attorney General Robert Kennedy, President Kennedy's brother, speaks about civil rights in 1963. He later became a senator and ran for president, but was assassinated in 1968.

Media coverage helped Americans see the truth about the injustices in the system. Cruel lawmakers were exposed. Presidents Kennedy and Johnson crafted legislation that protected equality.

Fannie Lou Hamer was a civil rights activist who worked tirelessly to register African-American voters. For this, she was fired from her job, shot at, arrested, and beaten by police. She never gave up.

Congress followed up by passing legislation that created laws to protect the ideals of the U.S. Constitution. Since then, new laws have been passed that protect individuals from unfair treatment due to race, gender, sexual identity, and religion.

An official portrait of President Barack Obama.

For many Americans, Barack Obama's election in 2008 was a manifestation of a lifetime of hoping for a better world. But the work for justice never really ends.

GLOSSARY

designated (DEZ-ig-nated): named or marked

eligible (EL-i-juh-buhl): having the rights or qualifications for something

forbade (fur-BADE): ordered not to do something

integrate (IN-ti-grate): to combine several things or people into one

mutilated (MYOO-tuh-lated): injured or damaged by disfiguring it

propel (pruh-PEL): to push something forward

retaliation (ri-tal-ee-AY-shun): the act of getting revenge or responding to attack or injury

rift (rift): a serious disagreement between people

segregated (SEG-ruh-gayt-ed): kept separate or apart

unanimous (yoo-NAN-uh-muhs): agreed on by everyone

INDEX

SHOW WHAT YOU KNOW

1. Name three ways in which people showed they disagreed with unfair policies.
2. Describe why Emmett Till's death had an effect on the country.
3. How did the Montgomery bus boycott make a difference?
4. Describe things ordinary people can do to bring change to their communities.
5. Do you think nonviolence is the best style of protest? Why or why not?

FURTHER READING

Adamson, Heather, *The Civil Rights Movement: An Interpretive History Adventure*: Capstone, 2016.

Zullo, Allan, *Ten True Tales: Young Civil Rights Heroes*: Scholastic, 2014.

Hooks, Gwendolyn, *If You Were a Kid During the Civil Rights Movement*: Children's Press, 2017.

ABOUT THE AUTHOR

Linden McNeilly is a writer who taught public school for many years. She loves writing about history, science, interesting places to go, and maps. She lives in the redwoods of California with her family and lots of pets. Visit her at www.lindenmcneilly.com.

www.rourkeeducationalmedia.com

Photo Credits: Shutterstock.com, istockphoto.com. Everett Historical-shutterstock.com COVER: Courtesy of United States Government; Pg4-5; Everett Historical, New York World-Telegram, A.R. Waud. PG6-7; Esther Bubley, Courtesy-The Library of Congress. PG8-9; Felix Lipov-shutterstock.com, The US National Archives. PG10-11; The US National Archives. PG12-13; The US National Archives, National Park Service. PG14-15; G. H. Farnum, Public Domain image. Pg16-17; cmh2315fl_flickr https://creativecommons.org/licenses/by-nc/2.0, WhisperToMe. PG18-19; The US National Archives, Public Image. PG20-21; Public Image, Courtesy-The Library of Congress, Courtesy National Archives. PG22-23; : Eege Fot vum -GNU Free Documentation License, Courtesy-The Library of Congress. PG24-25; : Carol M. Highsmith, Joon Powell- Creative Commons Attribution 2.5 Generic. PG26-27; Courtesy National Archives- Public Images. PG28-29; Calvin L. Leake | Dreamstime.com, Courtesy National Archives- Public Image. PG30-31; Gino Santa Maria- shutterstock.com, Courtesy National Archives- Public Image. PG32-33; Abbie Rowe -National Park Service, JFK Presidential Library-Public. PG34-35: Kheel Center, Cornell University -Creative Commons Attribution 2.0 Generic, Leffler, K. Warren, Rowe, Abbie, 1905-1967. PG36-37; : Chris Pruitt-Creative Commons Attribution-Share Alike 3.0 Unporte, Archives@dos.myflorida.com. PG: 38-39; : Kevin from Astoria, NY-Creative Commons Attribution 2.0 Generic, Courtesy-The Library of Congress, Public Image. PG40-41; : Richard apple -Creative Commons Attribution-Share Alike 3.0 Unported, Federal Bureau of Investigation, Bruce Davidson. PG42-43; Carol M. Highsmith, Rowland Scherman-USIA, Courtesy-The Library of Congress. PG44-45; Fernandez, Orlando, Courtesy National Archives- Public Image, National Park Service-Public Image.

Edited by: Keli Sipperley

Produced by Blue Door Education for Rourke Educational Media. Cover and Interior design by: Jennifer Dydyk

Living Through the Civil Rights Movement / Linden McNeilly
(American Culture and Conflict)
ISBN 978-1-64156-419-9 (hard cover)
ISBN 978-1-64156-545-5 (soft cover)
ISBN 978-1-64156-668-1 (e-Book)
Library of Congress Control Number: 2018930439

Rourke Educational Media
Printed in the United States of America, North Mankato, Minnesota